This book is perfect.

— *Susan Bright, Plain View Press*

Poets William Blake and ee cummings meet in Ric Williams' *the secret book of god*, but that's just the beginning of the sudden and slow ecstasies that will dance off the page into your head reading these poems. Intelligent bright fire, humor and love!

— *Chuck Taylor, PhD.*
Texas A&M University

Reading Williams' poems demands a fresh eye. It is necessary to read "differently," suspending not only preconceived definitions and expectations, but hanging suspended in negative capability realizing that the titles of the poems lie just as suspended at the ends of the lyric or sometimes narrative verse.

Connie Williams (no relation)
Forrest Fest Review

Sometimes brilliance reflects a pair of turning hands. To catch a glimpse of what this lovely brilliance is like suggests our own hands turn over pages of a book in which such secrets of soul-tending loveliness are shared. The book of poems by poet-mythologist Richard Lance Williams, *the secret book of god*, offers readers this kind of soulful opportunity. A remarkable and powerful expression of soul, *the secret book of god* can only be shared like a quest for the "mythogenic" center of our most deeply held knowing.

Stephanie Pope, MA
mythopoetry.com

the secret book of god

the secret book of god

by

Richard Lance Williams

Dalton Publishing   Austin, Texas

Dalton Publishing
P.O. Box 242
Austin, Texas 78767
www.daltonpublishing.com

© Copyright 2005, Ric Williams.
All rights reserved.

Some of these poems have appeared in various forms in the *Austin Chronicle, Creative Pulse Magazine*, or on the Web at *www.mythicartist.org*.

ISBN: 0-9740703-4-3
LCCN: 2005926715

Creative Design by Deltina Hay & Ric Williams

Printed in the United States of America by Alphagraphics, Austin, Texas. Cover: 100# Classic Linen Avon Bright White. Interior Pages: 70# Opaque.

in memory of my father

Table of Contents

[the way the women see what is radiant: an iron lotus]	11
[walking off]	13
[the reincarnation of moments]	14
[moving to where she will not be bound]	16
[revealing even these things]	18
[dreaming's memory]	20
[any moment begins with this]	21
[sun moon bear]	24
[resolved]	25
[what is holy]	27
[witness to wonder]	29
[god's name]	30
[fly fishing with master anglers of the deep]	31
[a conversation with Ramona, 11]	33
[craig doesn't like the word *arc*: or where are we]	35
[secret homes]	36
[when the dream bites into flesh]	38
[reaching for abraham]	39
[she said: you are a joyful man. you let everything belong.]	40
["imaginary cities: for rod amis"]	42
[taking in the light]	44
[quickly the dream in]	46
[rounding]	47
[i fall in love with clouds]	49
[the horizon beside you]	50
[wings—wings!]	51
[to claim the darkness of your shine]	52
[the wolf circle]	55
[i have known women . . .]	57
[some days]	58
[how we make of a moon everything]	59
[the fatness of the wyrm ouroboros]	61
[what do you hear when you leave]	63
[sober]	64
[dionysus in troy]	66
[dead edna]	67
[(as if red were red)]	68
[pollock alive/dead]	69
[the cranes]	73
[the *xynon* on the corner]	74
[the last time i heard her voice]	75

[the doors of heaven]	76
[instead of your flesh]	78
[a painted hook]	79
[how she carried his stars: navigating a loss]	82
[as if the wine resents the grape]	83
[more advice to a poet: just write]	88
[the dream of thin connection]	89
[identity]	91
[& there are emptinesses even tears cannot fill]	92
[a letter to some imagined self]	93
[she remembered an island]	95
[berries]	96
[what she wanted in clouds]	97
[end here]	99
[ten lines ringing]	100
[living in the valley]	101
[wants burning summer]	102
[nameless]	103
[having been seen]	104

" . . . all the true things must change . . ."

— *C. G. Jung*

Or if i lean in sometimes
the plastic just peels
off the tree & the
mountain cold
refuses this
hard blue

(whole of being)

melts like a
scream of
stones
in a
jar

(as if diamonds asked for rain)
(as if light were the gift of those who hide)

she said it was Pandora
& when i turned the lid it was only
because she asked me like an old woman
who wanted to see the dream of her son
the men under the table drinking
singing like seals like cold spits
of sea scum waving bright
shirts of siren treasure
as if the stars were
black rocks
burning
in her
heart

o melancholia
sweet body of Sir John's
Ophelia drowned in a dark pool
of what she could too well imagine

(these bruises of the soul like a gravity
heavy water holocaust maddening walls of iron)

the softness of decay
& she cannot leave but how she floats

her hands still open to the rain
of the impossible light

this weakness this nausea
the wretched roiling heat centered
in a space that cannot be located in the center
of this body imagined as another body inside this
mattered flesh the way she see things from the center of some
place both behind & before (yes—space::time)
this place sensed as face, as facing
how when she comes
here (this place)
neither head
nor throat
neither speech
nor thought
but this
poem
this place
winding
like a
river
ing
thru an
imagined body
this place that is between
what you see & what you cannot place
(those secret haunts where the ghosts sink down)

& if i held her hands & she spoke of some light thing
like the way a heart is a music that we can never understand

(what he cannot say is that he never wanted to understand anything)

what we want is something like the stone of the sun
when it has burned to its last grain
how it burned for all this
how it burned—

[the way the women see what is radiant: an iron lotus] f

Begin by walking & then the breath
i can't remember why they gave me the gift

of walking off

just beginning
just hitting the wall again &

as if i were to find a fallow field & make of it
a garden where birds swelled in blooms of star sap

a place where one bent & the sky unfolded

& the shine of a nail dug into a house
a small adobe square on the edge of a dream

the girl hangs her dress on the nail
& children pour out its pockets
pearls & apples & rivers

dropping from the quivering
tips of the pale green twigs

magnolias spinning in the turquoise air
& each time she smiles infinity curls inside

every sadness every scar a flower with an open mouth
ready to whisper, "again"

& this time she holds a cat & the driver waits to watch the women
adjust their hair in the window her eyes like that time

you walked into the field with the child laughing

where you remembered why the dream held more
than the memory of lost innocence

how dying can never diminish the wonder of a single breath
or the press of a hand on the face of a friend
how walking off is how the world begins

[walking off] f

Blind the cold February rain falls
    i come to this place seeing you
            turn in your white skin
                        shining

the years were another night of ivory combs
guessing which constellations skirted that moon
                        that tree line

where the lights like stars the way the rain fell onto the windshield

waiting for me to tell you to stop
            as if i were your heart

as if i held your mouth to the promise
        of a redemption only you could find when you
                finally stopped listening to someone like me

your eyes sadder than the painted box shaped like a bird of paradise
filled with your bobby pins & the feathers you brought me

relics of Eden you were already gone
            by the time the seer called me
                    into that trance of pharaohs & golden bell towers

the angels at my shoulder when the blade went in whispering
                            there is another way

how the voice came on a perfectly calm afternoon
       turning onto the driveway
           the butterfly in the branches
               of the tree line on that distant ridge

    the key dissolving
           there is nothing to fear she said
               & the butterfly landed on my shoulder
fluttered   once
          twice
              three times
                      before it lifted into blue memory

i have seen visions the prophets have seen
visions enough to have the nuns call me a liar
as i sat in the California hills watching fairies dance into the canyons

watching a man bleed to death

how the shadows left me with a golden fire & you in the colonel's jacket
driving away when i could not pull her name from the chamber
where the bone cut the night in two

i closed the window but the light still fell blinking in the shadows
like dying stars
like your fingers
when i said
let go

as you brushed my hair back
as if it were the hair of a child long dead

i'll see you again you said
i held to the night
like a ghost
afraid of
resurrection

you live in dreams
your flesh a light a skin
of rain of rivers pouring wisdom
a thousand years into a walk across the room

a room as wide as the distance
                between your hand on my chest
                              & what tenderness could not see

[the reincarnation of moments] *f*

As if the will
of a single hand
a twiggish finger

a point of a consequent stick
drawn through the dirt of kings

(this domain & no others)

the architects of sleep design the world
lacing moments like foam at the edge of every now

a silk thread horizon
a bride's slip slipping
unmade as soon as made

a trick of Penelope's

memory loosening the false inheritance

an island trance sinking

he judges in another depth
   all the riches at your feet
& still were but a single bird to lose its way
   in this night of long migration

   he would bend in shame
      the ring unwhole
         no light to strike save the light burning
           in the depthless soul

— fragile beauty —

brittle as frost on a naked field

     what moves us to invisible needs

— unheard —
— untouched —

she goes to it again & again
   a salt lick
     a wound
        a haunted well

the long silence like years poured from a single vase of

— closed intention —

a garden where passion does not unwind like the helix of a rose

he pruned them for forty years
    & still he never learned to cut away

his need to cut

      — quietly —
      — cold —

as she struggled to unfold
falling year by year into the dry line of leaving
her heart dissolving as he pointed to the lime white sky

the birds
    already lost
        in the redness of sinking into
            the fallow fields of his hard heaven

[moving to where she will not be bound] *f*

Mountains & saints & stars
   carved into the mountains
     the sun in your hands
      the mountain
      — your younger brother —
        waiting for the blessing
      — your broad hand —
         upon its glistening skin

he makes his way through a tangle of leaves
finds himself at the edge of a river
— the plains of a bright seeing —

        slipping away to the west

(there is no time
  but direction —
    if he said
      tomorrow
       he could be dead)

a fiction of the functionalists

    (we could think ourselves
      back to the womb
       given enough time)

the struggle is no less magnificent
  — if the man is a man —
    — if the mountain is a mountain —
      — if the stars are stars —

or are they artifacts of a question?

    what is the authenticity of epiphany

      art is not it
     artifacts are not it
    remembering is not it
  beyond the miracle lies something other
  — what lies beyond the experience —

    you look
           & there are
                the stars
                    the mountains
                        the sun — a figure that might be
                                                you

something beyond
        the dream

some
      thing

to speak in a language
                    beyond words   or images   or thought

                an authenticity
                      of being
                          behind the light
                              revealing

even these things
as it does not
reveal

itself

[revealing even these things] *f*

Or perhaps we are dreams manifest
living dreams backwards
peripherally sidereally
as it were the stars
not telling our fortune

but we theirs
perhaps we are to dreams
what landscapes are to us
they belong to us no more than
what wind can claim on sky

sometimes i think to act
is merely to be driven
by forces as invisible
as the pleasures
of aging hearts

what draws me to blue
to the green eyes
sadly smoking
in the dark
of dreams

what happiness hones its edge
on my ransomed flesh
as if to remember
was to be
remembered

o, these dreams dreaming us
these acts of will falling
in a time measured
between dreams
& dreaming's long
unwinding memory

[dreaming's memory] *f*

Poems like a series of breaths
like the parts of a tree
the bark to the leaf
to the flower
the pollen
the wind
to the skin
of the infinite
glistening with stars

(you're funny, she laughs)

like a moment in a life
each distinct yet
one is connected
to the previous
to the next
the first to
the last

(how we begin anywhere
it being no different than any
beginning in an infinity: in your mouth: a word)

every held breath

(the blue of this heaven
the water always with ribbons
inside the bowl of flesh
the way you float
with the sun
the ghosts
of every
folding
wave)

every gasp

(how when it feels
as if you hold
the world
encircled
twice)

back to the quickening
a quickening
of sperm
to egg

the heartbeat built
of breaths taken
by the mother
the father
& back,
back

this series
of quickenings
how every poem
radiates from a center

the heart

the beginning
everywhere
radiates
in all directions
through all times
only one time the moment

every moment

the multitudinous hearts
centering
now

the Tao
the center
no moment
other than the eternal now

the connected heart
the beauty the truth
of each moment
simultaneous
creation

pick a poem
any poem

a heart
any heart

(how beautiful she is:
naked smiling
her right breast
cupped in her own hand)

an old woman laughing

saying:
any moment
begins with this

[any moment begins with this] *f*

The rivers insist on my feet
how the water gives me
a mark on the wall
sacrifice she tells me
is what happens
in every breath
& what i hate
more than you telling me
you will not close this door
until all the world is a light

i will only bend in the river
when the bears come
down into the
spring to taste

the flesh of the trout
caught in the pools
like suckered suns

the early morning
when you sat
in the white
of this world

& breathed as if there
were nothing
to believe
but your eyes

your eyes & my hands
cupping your face saying

this is where the moon was born

you in the river
looking over your shoulder

as i wrestled with a fish like a legless bear

[sun moon bear] *f*

If i could take back a single word
a gesture a glance a held breath
if the moon would hang a little longer
   between those leaves
those gorgeous trembling leaves

his body so still
i squeezed his hand again
we tested his strength each day
stronger now
less so now
we would look into
each other's eyes
i would say yes
he would hold
my eyes to gauge
my concern
but whatever he saw
he'd always say
we'll make it
he laughing
she saying he looked real good
he wanted to know what strings
we pulled to be so fresh
i wanted to know his blood sugar count
what he ate
how much
what day it was
where he was
& most days he had no idea
of any of that
he'd smack his lips
ask me to bring buttermilk
ask me where'd i been for so long
but we had that handshake
more even than the kisses
than the stroking of his fine hair
he knew what we were testing
more than strength
more than strength
he would never give up
even unto death

& when i saw the body
the first thing i did
was squeeze his hand
blood poured
from the right side
of his mouth
i wiped it with a tissue
put the tissue in my pocket
it is still there

even as i write this poem

that night the moon held the gold
the sun pressing to find the depth of stars

even as i held back
forgetting the stone grip of his resolute heart

[resolved] *f*

Consciousness as phenomenon
engendering consciousness in the inanimate

(where does that circle begin)

the ordering of stones
of wood
of plastics
engenders
by our ordering
a consciousness
a consciousness in them

(is this truth)

this wall of hand—piled rocks
ensouled
as against a pile of rubble
tumbled by a quake

or how quiet the stone
how amenable it is to lie
or roll
or hold a bridge
rest at the bottom of a lake
pulled by surge of tide
or pushed by the wedge
of a stretching glacier
out for a millennial stroll

how do you write on lightning
measure the stone's consciousness
the film of memory of genetics of quickening

where is it stored
what tattoo—carving—press
cut in the space
between electrons
between synapses
bridges this
particular color

with that peculiar
turn of a hand
on that specific day

how is memory written
in a photon's trough

consciousness is inexplicable
so i choose to engender stones
with the same reverence as i would this poem

    no less than the voice it engenders

[what is holy] *f*

Already the evening & they speak their parts & pass into the stars
i applaud them & imagine some dark pool beyond the lawn
a silvery skin breaking pale blue where a woman floats
alone in a field of colored lights in a city unnamed
& still i do not know the world
but stand entranced
as the stars fade
knowing i have
just arrived
to gaze on you
sparkling in that pool
even as i have nothing to say

[witness to wonder] *f*

I have more need to call the names of god
look in the phone book
& there is nothing but names of god
& if i could know
what the grackle calls its young
i would hear more names of god
& what each cloud calls its neighbor
& the name of that hill
that bush that tree that leaf
what name each stone has
for the bed it lies on
for the particular wind
that cools it each evening
that warms it at noon
what is that wave of light
playing just there on your cheek
what is your lips' name
the one god whispers
each time you speak

[god's name] *f*

Henri matisse the beautiful man
who picasso proclaimed as the only one
(& what he meant by that was that henri was
THE artist incarnate)
& what henri offered
on the source of his art
design & line & color & space
lemons & stars breasts legs & hands
was that when he did not know what a painting meant
that when he came to a place he did not know
this was the place where art was born
to not know what this means
to not know why this line
this place
this gesture done twice
this pattern this color washed again
to not know but still follow
where the unknown beauty led . . .

all we know is that this
thing we do not know
is beautiful
it is
inexplicably
beautiful
& that what is vital
is inexplicable
that what is inexplicable
is vital
is the mystery that deepens
with our sorrow
& our joy
that refuses our arrogant attempts
to bring the wondrous
the beautiful
to heel

cut the leash
follow the flame

pablo learned to fish
studying in the shadows

where the great henri
dropped his lines

fish every day
he taught
good days & bad
like a poet
just writing
throwing out lines
wood on the fire of imagination
& what he offers his guests
whether raw or cooked
still requires first
lowering the line into the unseen
the unknown
the pull
& then the scaling the boning
the placing on a plate
& even if he simply
ties a string to his toe
& dreams by a shallow pool
the tastiest of meals always requires
knowledge of fire & a knife

[fly fishing with master anglers of the deep] *f*

Waiting for the ferry she asks
how did land separate from water
& why isn't the sky a sea & the sea a sky
i smile & say the clouds are a sea wandering in heaven
waiting for a ferry to bring them back home
& she laughs asking why there are more
taxis in New York City than here
& i laugh & offer that perhaps
more people long for a home
in the loneliness of NYC

(& the pelicans on the
harbor posts watch
the dead fish
float on
the gray
water)

if we step on a cloud would we
fall straight down, she presses
would you fall right through
the water if you walked
on it, miss question
well, then why do
dead fish float
& why aren't
the clouds filled
with dead birds

(& why can a man
hear a voice
before it cries)

after a silence
i fall to watching ants
& she says, do ants help each other

if they find one drowning
no, i say, that's not
how ants work

do they just
eat each other
when they die

is that why rain falls
to be eaten by the ocean
eaten by the land that left it

do dreams wait for us
to eat them with our words
& let them float on our memory

(& years from now will she ask
daddy, are you really there
floating in my memory)

[a conversation with Ramona, 11] *f*

N ine geese winging west
   following the river

  i
s x

tw
  o

one

the space between a commentary
do i need to spell it out

  i
s x

tw
  o

one
how the wind pushes

the one
harder on the same line

mcmurtry spoke of mountains of buffalo bones
how an old Indian walked & walked for days

stephanie tells me we'll have to find a new word for where we are, or when

[craig doesn't like the word *arc*: or where are we] *f*

How we speak of things in secret
the tongues of water
washing us back
to ecstasy

where the moon leaves the wall of heaven
& drapes itself like a face on your belly
arching a back under dark trees
its fingers like rivered stars

(folly of imagination
to take an eye
make of it
a ghost)

(memory sees things that passed
like ships between a whirlpool
& a maw of clashing rocks
the desires of loneliness)

a secret of home
of beginnings
of ghosts
of lies

a philosophy of turns
the architects who
give me flesh
& dreams

you want my hands on your breasts
i want my breasts in the sea
in a heart like a dance
of stars melting

what can we bring from the sea
that is not found in the moon
or in the olive trees
waiting for you

an etymology of secret flowers
of home & the eye closing

even as it begins to see
what desire opens

odysseus shaman strapped to the mast
did you hear what the mermaids
whispered between their song
how love lives on dreams

how the secret is an ache
of the wood for the sea
the sea for the clouds
the clouds for falling

(some say the moon is a lonely water
waiting for the sea to call its
name but the sea has lost
its tongue to all of us)

whoever can find the sense of love
can find a home in any land
can break the ghostly hold
& know the cost of ash

[secret homes] *f*

If the endless
light of eternity
feels like
that bone
protruding
from my wrist
i'll take
the wrappings
of time poured
from a rusty
colored bottle
of laudanum
& count the end
of dreams
an orgasm
worth
the scream

[when the dream bites into flesh] *f*

This reaching for that place
this reaching for a core
as if after all these tricks
all these brilliant twists
& dodges & nods of
approval passing this
test & that one as if
as if every one of my
dreams were a clue
were a bread crumb
dropped by myself
invisibly one step ahead
leading me into this
place where the wondrous
joy beyond all myth awaits
as if there is one last
epiphany & then the walls
dissolve & waves of applause
the greetings of the gods
& a floating a big comfortable
chair a beer & children asleep
in my lap & i close my eyes
& there i was all along
you holding my hand
as if you had known exactly
where we were going at every breath

[reaching for abraham] *f*

It only seems as if there is no real choice
as if the very miracle of being
has to encompass
what cannot
be encompassed
what breaks
what hurts

he embraced a man today
who despised his politics
because he could not tell
him any other way
that ideas must always
give way to the heart
if the heart says make way

& he watched a program
where white baby birds
forced a younger
brother from the nest
to the waiting jaws
of a crocodile
& he wanted to cry

& he was happy
the shrinking crocodiles
had something to eat
that they had found
a tree of life where
heaven's quarrels
deepened the sea

& these are simple things
utterly unprofound
as quotidian as bird shit
as breaking waves
on a rocky shore
as loneliness on
this empty beach

he always had his
loneliness for company

his fear & doubt
such sweet companions
the one's who would not come
were always there with his sorrow
a constant joy knowing he came from two

& what would the artist say
the philosopher the hard mad monk
the warrior with his crocodile teeth
his feathers & his statistics in a claw
a cultural indigestion of fits & starts
we will all make way when the door opens
when the light pours in & our lips part as if to say

[she said: you are a joyful man. you let everything belong.] *f*

This image of a woman (a man)
this other half of me
who does not want
what i want
but needs to be heard
seen felt believed
because i am two
when i am not more
or a lesser thing unlived
yet living
unformed
but unfolding
like a day on the other side of sunrise
somehow we must find a ritual that assuages
her hurt (his pain) the absence that is always with us
honor it without sacrificing the tenderness of our own flesh
an ounce of flesh & not one drop of blood
if it were only blood
a letting a bleeding
that seems so less than flesh
as if slow enough
(make haste slowly)
i could bleed forever
the vampire other
satisfied with the drip of
my blood & yet it too
cannot suffice
as if the spirit
as if whatever is foremost
calls to the hindmost
earth to sky
male to female
joy to sorrow
a dance from bank to bank
the river bottoms
as deep as the surface is long
i offer this
you want that
how can i find a bundle of bones
wrapped in a skin
& call it my soul
rituals worked for some
ten thousand years

a way to tell the demons no
to answer yes to angels
to offer something more & less
of who you can only imagine
is who you would be
in the roundness of the others
say you will pay no more of your flesh
that these words are the offering
& the other must find some succor in them
i don't know what else to say except yes
to the marriage of all that is & was & will be
waiting in the emptiness that can never be filled
except with imaginary cities imagining how you will undress them
imagining how *you* are a different *you* in different cities in different times
how the cities change as these energies ebb & flow
dreaming each other into new existences . . .
"No one, wise Kublai, knows better than you
that the city must never be confused with the words that describe it."
Italo Calvino in *Invisible Cities*

["imaginary cities: for rod amis"] *f*

The way the boy nervously sits in the boat
with his hands on either rail
his eyes taking in the light
like it is the only light
in the wide world
the sun not yet up
birds quiet as
the king floats in the water
staring coldly at the last remaining stars
the boy's father whispering from the shore

this fish will speak when the birds heal the air

it is always this way & the door to his office opens
the numbers rolling out like small balls of shit
hefted by dung beetles with coin slot heads
accountant fish swimming in a flat lake
burning in the stench of a green fire

how do you breathe he asks one
its gills a gas flame blue
whistling under the weight
of a tight equation

the fish bubbles a boiling algorithm
it is the ten fold light of summer falling
(the year of blind crabs clacks on the temple's sea walls
schools of salt caked saviors walking games in slippers of glass)

these same keys
where Galileo
denied his eyes
dualism is born again
atomistic solar flare a hook

we deny it is all a shell
a wall so thin the energy spinning
a boat a scale a skin of water a father
what lies on his back in a dry bed shining
like a tooth on fire

she says "you always go to the fish"
the boy rattles the oar rings
the oars were not the memories he could hold
chemicals do not remember a loss of her wanting

what would you extract if the fear would say, "step out . . . let go . . .

drift

   into the land where nothing counts

      but everything
         you never doubted

not even when you saw a bird in a cage

its face exactly like the way she cupped your face taking in the light

[taking in the light] *f*

Or what we find
the little snake
the offered
bird that sickens us
because we must eat
what we cannot forsake
how the horrible draws us in
or abandons us to what we would find wanting

[quickly the dream in] *f*

& this she knows
the first word sets
the key as in a
piece of
music

(we are *here*)

the second note
pulls us in the degree
that sets this trajectory

(we are heading into *this* roundness)

so the beginning
before a first
must be an
approach
a prayer
an offering
a silence that still speaks

(open a little liquid sea
& we will do the rest)

*what if all you had to do
was—open a little—
& let the light*

*spill out—into this flesh —
this hour—this trace*

of our eternity

or how i cannot thank
you enough for
sharing who
you are

& when i am with you
i feel like i am in

a cathedral
& yes i
am & yes i know
how you cramp &
wheeze & lie sometimes
in extraordinary pain & long
to be seen as the person who lives
behind that frame of flesh
but can never be seen so
clearly as those times
when but by grace
a light falls upon
a sentence or a
look or a small
& transitory
gesture . . .

so thank you
the one who
cannot be seen
tender & deeper
than any scattering light

& how the silence rounds us

   [rounding] *f*

I fall in love with clouds
the rain that was your water
the snow that was your tears
the hail that was your anger
the sleet of my sorrow
how you live in the rivers
of my islanded heart
the ghosts of falling
in love forever
against the blue
of what i lost
to heaven

[i fall in love with clouds] *f*

(How the moonlight of rivers
solves resistance)

return this day

(or should she fall
stealing the light of her longing)

floating in a field of bitterweed

(pressing layers of a slow gain
a white on blue: watching birds mate in rain)

this incremental interiority: life has no front or back

(how memory breathes beside you like an endless wall every life
a life in parallel: your ghosts throbbing like a nerve code)

what we press is neither past nor present but walks with us folding depth

(Hephaestus slaving for love in Poseidon's palace of waves dreaming star
legged floors: a cloth of oldest weave—a net of infinite presence)

the river like a nimbus stripped of any face save this one that holds us
forever in reflection

[the horizon beside you] f

Wings—wings!
this a heaven caged

steel lattice holds against
throatings of smoky prayers
curling tendrils wrapping pinions

up—up!
watch them climb

who eyes these gray undoings
grip of breakaway plateaus—intimation
power slips the desperate cords of a knotted land

a foothold like a lobster fluttering at the edge of Picasso's eye

see thru the grid of all that maps carry
a plan of layers (mud sheet topos)
thin as a devil's skin of lies

how we fall in our own lost sky
like rain on bloody feathers

[wings—wings!] *f*

Yes, yes, she curls
into the shape of a seed
how i must come to the hard god

Hades, triune ruler, son of Kronos
Polydegmon, the receiver of guests
the giver of wealth: a terrible visage

(the waters belong to him:
stare into their surface & see his face)

still & invisible & the source
in the very center
of everything

(Dionysus
harrowing
the regretful
the unripened will)

his halls the bowels of the earth
the hidden wealth you have
not tapped averting your
eyes at gifts you dare
not claim for fear
of who you are:

(he tears such
illusions apart:

who lies they would
not give their fears
to render the
treasure
of their
heart:

he takes them
suddenly in
Eleusis)

gold sapphires oil
the dark richness
of the grain

how the roots
reach as far down
into the cool moist soil
as they reach into the hot dry air

here the ghosts roll their shoulders
(where are the wings you refused to spread)
fall apart decay into the elements of fire & hard truth

how the lightness
(o, naive Persephone)
is cured of her gathering

becomes the gathered
the Queen of Eternity

let the demons witness your descent
follow them where they lead
entertain them; what they
say; what they have
always said in a
truth you had
to refuse until
refusal fell
ready to
change

until the bottom
au fond became
a spring

he who receives guests

be received

the roundness of the world
is the darkness & the light
the shine in bitter blood

the sweetness of dying
to a truth of who you
held out to become

or if he cupped your breasts
so you might feel
the fullness
of your
time

[to claim the darkness of your shine] *f*

Wolves
guardians of heaven
companion to apollo lykios
a guide through the darkness
the chthonic companion mother

(demon, glutton, aggressor
cloak of hades, deceiver—
see persephone
pulling flowers
laughing
her lips
so red
how innocent is the maiden
when she hesitates in the shadows)

what logic says the palimpsest
of death life death life
the stone slow to
water the water
slow to stone

pulled moment to moment
guided by the mad
hunger for this
heaven that
tells you now
is now
& now
& now
& what lie
would you have her
lead to your door
when what
you want
is to drop
each flower
at the feet of love
& say no more
when all you want
is more
even if you were

to stop
& you will
not stop
because the hunger
was the turning
toward the light
the hunger
was leaving
that moment
& that moment
& so the wolf is there
this moment
this hunger
saying what lie
would you have me tell
to say i am not here
you are not here
you are not
beloved
when everything
in your wanting
puts the lie
to your
belief
in your
own death

all you can follow is the hunger
the light the hot close breath
upon your glorious face

the death belongs
to someone else

[the wolf circle] *f*

Her fingers like tendrils flit before her
like a blind woman reading
the sad history of air . . .

how does one become a good human
how can you forgive yourself
for an unhealed wound . . .

i remember her alone in an airport
the bright yellow of Mexico
a crushing loneliness . . .

where are you when you fall apart
who dissolves inside the cup
where you hold beauty . . .

she is more lovely than she imagines
she is closer to god than angels

& the waters sing . . .

even as she hides like a flower—
inside her moon of tears

even as she breaks . . .

[i have known women . . .] *f*

&
some days
only crying will do

or a knife & a long hill

to plunge the blade
of all that can't be said
into the side of that which hides
the roof of persephone's prison palace

some days to knock on persephone's doors . . .

she who knows what it is to be taken

by what will not yield

& then the tears

& then

some days

as if the gold of all that processed bitterness
were no more than a daydream
pulled sullenly into the sun

forgiveness
yet another sin
hiding in the taken hand

& then

the barrows

shame

& a long, long knife

[some days] *f*

Or if i were filled
with shards
until she poured
them from my mouth

how the chogak po pojagi
(the word for wrapping cloths
made from left-over scraps
of woven silk thin silk
rough ramie hemp
torn cotton
sorrow)
the exquisite needlework
of poor Korean women
repressed by Three
Tenets of Obedience
Chosun Dynasty
(1392 to 1910)
confined even
in their homes
to an inner
room

(o, Ms. Woolf
there are rooms
& there are rooms)

as if 1911 brought
relief as if
when i
woke
the stars
hid their faces
because of my shame

how this work anticipated
the fractured paintings
of Mondrian Picasso
Klee the modern
iconoclasts of
this West

or is loneliness ever
anticipated
& how
we push small
stones into a circle

& when you die
the lies sewn in your soul
the fears that wrapped your heart
dissolve like dust inside a lover's bath

[how we make of a moon everything] *f*

Fish snake dream
immortal new skin
bearded king sleepy blond
women greet the stranger with the veil

hold my white thighs open
let the wounds feed the sun
follow the long beach where the gods arrive

(note: write a business plan—humiliate all souls—
begin with ambition with a mission to save the world from snakes)

whose dreams play the beast
where does imagination begin
presume it is all for god's belly

(kindness is a measure we bleed
while praying against the inevitable turn of the plan—
this too is the inner curve of the serious bloom)

how many snakes like stars curled in the wintered cut
(dig a gray hole for roses, ditch the banks of the nile)

chartered streets the ripples of time god calling in her chips
the forest a field a road a village a ruin a feast of stones

(do you expect a profit from a loss
none of this is real—ask parmenides,
buddha, your metaxic noe,
but don't ask your heart)

intention a bitter cloud on the lip of a grave
(see the angels dancing like harridans)
the mourning seeps up
the evening settles
nothing

out of the void a vapor
like the light of a river
a dream, a dream

(how is it different
than your knees)

if i took you in my mouth
your soul a hook made
of my desire

(whose business is the wrapped sorrow,
the sudden smile imagined again)

my mouth an answer
for your penetrating eye

you belong in my mouth
i belong in your eye

both of us on our knees
our bellies in the dream of god

[the fatness of the wyrm ouroboros] *f*

The cicadas & mockingbirds trade opinions
like shrill philosophers

long blue stretches of cloud tatter
float between sine waves
like tabled heat

(it is all a music of heaven)

where is this fisheye of consciousness
a silence like a broken window

dead flies peppering a rounded floor
swelled in the ghost wind of
abandoned plains

(the phone rings
but no one is
on either
end)

[what do you hear when you leave] *f*

Drunk the night fronted us the sweet madness we'd tamped
into the calluses of the days' blinding slights
we played with knifes better in the dark
our lives brighter in the shadows
where we are not hounded
by the tailor joke of tuck
here pull there tilt hold
fold squeeze pucker
bend hunch drop
dead

drunk the night
they came all bright
floating on star gravel

we watched as if we were apes in a cage
this road ends in a waterfall

i don't know how to write poems
they leaned into the next room
the room in tomorrow

gray sky sliding on gray hills
like steps a hundred years wide

they ran down laughing
like women when the ships
sail away & the new wine flows
    like a dream of rain

we kept losing time
they were naked standing in the lake
but we were lost Arthurs drunk on Artaud & ice
of what the meaning of existence had to do with existence

how do you say they were there but not there
how they were one nanosecond beyond our flesh
how we saw them only through some quirk of space/time
    without eyes

how they saw us without light
told us without words

how could we be
exactly who we were
since we were not there anymore
except we were still as lost as the fabled Excaliber

they were leaning into us thirty years away & already i was leaning back

still out of sync

how drunk the night fronted us the madness we could not bear
in the day with our calluses of slights

we play with knives better in the dark
cut the hems of the lace jackets

become who we are not who we are not promised to be
but who they saw when we fell screaming into the falls

who were those boys who walked that road
who lay beside those bright shadows & claimed their lives
        full with bellies & hard flesh

i do not know how to write poems of transcendent truth
but once i witnessed a man drown in a river with a woman he loved
& they looked like angels whose lives were brighter in the shadows
        than mine in this held light

[sober] *f*

Dionysus squats in the smoldering ruins of the white city
drawing loose circles with a blackened twig
this is troy three days after the burning
cassandra's ghost weaving in the thinning smoke
dionysus smiling his head tilted like a broken wheel
tell them, cassandra, that heaven does not exist
tell them that hell is a town in texas
new york is thirsty & the girls want gin
steel bends as readily as the truth
dionysus leading us through the dark jungles
the goats with their long wool
staring by the mountain cave
someone gave her a bouquet
bird of paradise & dark poppy
i want these lives of trouble to sail like
my eye seeing through circled fingers
an island where madness huddles
in a dark cold snow
with a fire like a beast
burning
dionysus squatting
the twig a meander
cutting new rivers
in the concrete dust
cassandra
sleeping
dreamlessly

[dionysus in troy] *f*

These spring leaves
　how many in this tree
that stands outside dead Edna's place

do they hear Ramona ask what is a poem

what does that mean
i do not want to go to school today
i want to play with these bugs with their big shadows

her face red with running
dead Edna never spoke to us
i've seen her ghost in the way Ramona looks like lonely girls

Judith knows who strokes old cats
counts the one she has buried in the garden
all the moments the sun caught in a young girl's face

& revealed a young woman with her hands outstretched

pretending to sleepwalk
into being an old ghost woman
who knows every time a bug shook silk from a spring morning

every leaf a universe
a hundred thousand leaves just there behind the creek
& i cannot hold my girl a single moment without seeing my beauty

walking on a red—leafed road with me & Edna silent in the trees

[dead edna] *f*

As if logic & faith were interchangeable
as if blue were red (as if red were red)
as if the machinery of modernity
were matted clots of jealous dreams
pulled from a monkey's ass

(as if red were red)

as if a thousand miles
or a thousand years
or the torch of the sun
could not relieve us
of all this aching distance

[(as if red were red)] *f*

P ollock was crazy
   crazy alive
nuts kookoo
oogily boogily
crazy alive
& he saw
he SAW
he saw it all
saw clean through
saw how to make paintings
that are alive
alive!
that if you look at them now
even now
they are still alive
alive like a coil of snakes
like a tangle of electrified wires
like a net of firing neurons
he is dead
but the paintings are alive
he is kaput
blew it all out
nuts
he was nuts
because he SAW
saw how to make paintings alive
make them breathe
make him dance like that
like look look
nothing dances like that
not like that
like paintings alive
go to the painting!
look
see through to how a man
made paint live
how he touched
the electrical aliveness
that shoots through everything
every thing
how he wrote it down
wrote on lightning
& laid it down of canvas

made love to it
until it came to life
& it's alive
it's alive & he's dead
it killed him
killed him
because he SAW
like looking at the atomic bomb
saying holy mother of god damn
& slowly slowly backing away
step by step
what have we done
broken the codes
smashed the tablets
& we backed away
but pollock
pollock
he didn't back away
he did it all
did what shelley's frankenstein
only dreamed of doing
what every artist dreams of doing
create life
create something that is
the very essence of life
not merely code
no watson & crick crack DNA
cadeusus extrapolation
gregorian hand job
but to be the finger of god
to spark that arc of electricity
to be that electricity
pole to pole
to feel the quickening
o christ o prometheus strapped to the sun
pollock did it
& here we are 30 years after
i told my minimalist revolutionaries
that after pollock there
was nothing to do but go backwards
but we can't believe
we can't stop living
but the light of that civilization

flashed its super nova in 1948
& though we now paint with electricity
with microchip numbers
(oh god we paint with numbers)
we use rude machines
dance like wired frog legs
to miracles we do not understand
that distance us from creation
from magic
the magic
pollock did it straight
straight stoned drunk crazy
with canvas & colored oil
with the blood of earth
he willed chaos alive
he SAW through the seemingness of things
to the bare subtextual electric reality
the light of consciousness
the improbable fire
that bears all meaning
because he SAW like moses
threw the light down
threw it onto the canvas
with the wholeness of his flesh heart & soul
& he made it alive
a commandment to see
the ALIVENESS of it ALL
challenges us to endow every thing
we do with that consciousness
no matter how ugly
how outrageous
how prickly the forest
of our mad mad needs
see it SEE it
see it ensouled
let the fire of
JACKSON POLLOCK
the fire of being
CRAZY ALIVE
to a light
imbued with a mystery
that only deepens

as it reveals
crazy crazy
immortal life
pollock calls you
TO LIVE
in that light
because
that light
is YOURS!

[pollock alive/dead] *f*

We folded a thousand cranes
   & still he died
we chanted a thousand prayers
& still he died
we threw a thousand coins
into the sunrise ocean
& still he died
we wept & wept
a thousand days
& when he died
someone said
a cloud has carried
his gleaming soul
into our hearts
& now he lives
inside you
with a thousand cranes
& a thousand prayers
a thousand copper coins
& tears enough to remember how
love holds the days
of a thousand broken hearts
& still there are the stars to fill
with the light of our unbreakable love

[the cranes] *f*

"...the symbols express the experience that man is fully man by virtue of his participation in a whole that transcends his particular existence, by virtue of his participation in the *xynon*, the common, as Heraclitus called it . . . "
— Eric Voeglin, *Modernity without Restraint*

Woman on clutches in pale blue velour short
shorts blond hair cropped at her neck
pink cotton top no shoes
her back to the west
swaying at the bus stop
saturday evening speed of connection
the thin lightning in the south
cracks on the thick gray
wall of hail—laced
cold rain like a
yellow vein
throb

philosophers pick up the golden artifacts of their mad wrestling
in the void of god like sailors entranced strange souvenirs
slipped to them in the ghostly abyss on which floats
the thousand petaled lotus & in the lotus
shiva dreaming philosophers sailing

(newton's law jetsam a failure to penetrate the dream)

"behold" they exclaim displaying their work
as if they were its source & we all fondle the creatures
like fish fallen from heaven: mathematics physics chemistry law

a green sedan pulls up
she pulls her shorts to the side
"lookee here" she coos
the face of a man—
thinking pussy
& there it is
as if philosophy
were no more than the evolution of lightning
dreaming of the wetness in a gray throbbing stone

[the *xynon* on the corner] *f*

Her voice is the canyon
the river that cut it
a flower an ocean
a mouth a moon
an eye whose glance
like a lock
opens or closes
the ruins
to the memory
of tourists
who did you believe
where were the fires
when the women ran
naked into the church
weeping for the knife
i shrink into a secret
a shame where i watch
my numbness eat my heart
stare me in the eye
flaunting my cruelty
my cold stupidity
as if blankets of snow
were a gift of red grace
hiding in the night
the truth of nakedness
we wander blinded crazed
a shaggy goat in a final light
the shards of the first regret
some lattice of false intent
where watery ghosts
like a mildew cling
to the gilded walls of paradise
we only wish to separate
like rain from cloud
this chamber of falling
as hard as ambition
a voice silent
as proud
what is shameful
is only what we refuse to love

[the last time i heard her voice] f

I sat on a couch writing
when a japanese woman
all in black with black makeup
severe bangs
& chopped hair
at the base of her neck
unsmiling, walked
into the lobby of a music school
& waited for the piano teacher
to bring her son
from his lessons
she never made eye contact
with anyone
& of course i know
the tradition of
the unsmiling
japanese
nobility
but instead
i felt
this mask she wore
(i imagined a stone
smoothed by a river
for a thousand years)
as one of resolute
negated resignation
to a world of men
(& women)
who were forever
hoping for that
electric spark
that quickening
of recognition
of a lover
of a god
of an opening
to another world
another dimension
a vision
an epiphany
how the gaze

(voyeur
predator
prey)
seeks
rescue
seeks escape
or entrance
a magic passage
through the eyes
of another
into yourself
& yet
how tiresome
it must become
being seen as a doorway
& not as heaven itself

[the doors of heaven] *f*

Instead of your flesh
(there is only this flesh)
instead of your heart
(where else would she sleep)
instead of your spirit
(how else are there stars)
instead of your energy
(when will you touch
the water still breathing)
we talk ourselves into a stubborn silence
our logic quivering like a fish on a stick
we take a cloud & let it wander on our skin
drawn by the imprint of a mother's imagined grief
(each rose—colored cheek an invitation to a bloody loss)
ten thousand years of children dead by the age of 10
how many times can we cut the cord
how many lovers' best intentions
shrink to a calloused thumb
on the lips of a slaughter
never slacked

when you stood at the window naked to the world
& the curtains were a light lent to the moon
why did the heavens blame you
for wanting what they refused to claim
as if falling were not answering a secret pride

[instead of your flesh] *f*

She paints a hook

(how the artist/priest takes it
& builds a city of eyes:
the Argos
the seeing
the seen
the hanging god
the meat of Inanna
the crown the diadem
the soft sweet tear of a woman's sex)

or if the bridge where the dream
asks the well: what is your dead father

the wanting mouth on an Egyptian watching the pyramids tower
watching it grind down a ground of ghosts

(which memory
do you capture
in the net of
forgetting
as if it were
leviathan
as if there were
no pity in the world
no pity in this world
for the insatiably hungry)

each stranger on the street

(the streets of Paris Rome
London Paradise Oz)

like a figure of a frieze in an Exodus of light
a child in an empty room switching the magic lamp

on & off
on & off

the two strands
mean memory begins

(a string theory
a rope bridge singing)

a pulse remembers the wave
memory held tightly in the vault of eternity

(nothing is forgotten)

when will i become only (again) a concept
in a filament (o, string)
of thought (too late)

the pleroma is already full
(all debts are paid)

or if you look closely
(a god so immense, so inherent)
& breathe like attar of rose (an essence)
how even the ash
of a bum's
cigarette
(or Powhatan
or Walter Raleigh)
falls as elegant as a mountain
or the last spar of Melville's Pequod
glittering in a setting sun (o, red eagle; o, eye)

or the crested cranes
rising thru the screening
mists of a river's silver morning
the cool wet air a dragonfly kissing
the skin of a pregnant lake

how the ripples of her skirt twirl
or my finger hooked
in the loop of her
nestlike hair

(who paints this moment just for you
trembling beyond existence—a wanting world

or if a bridge where we wake as a child
or a ghost rustling in the reeds

curling a long blue light

how the brush of Vermeer hung there
waiting waiting

[a painted hook] *f*

What her eye sees guided by
a trembling hand set to center

pull through twice
twice again

the raven with the gold ring in its beak
(is this you carrying your own nature)

the ice clouds waiting for the breath of the open eye
(see how you enter the shadows of your own forsaken heart)

the empty boat like a button on the coat of a dying man
rising & lowering as the long sea settles in the broken brass bed

a man is blind to the stars the gods have claimed
for only stars in the black connections of his own emptiness can carry him

these tears flying to the center & seeing the round cry of your dark dreaming
as it seeps through the cracks in the hands placed like stones on your face

[how she carried his stars: navigating a loss] *f*

R ilke said in the first
duino elegy
"for beauty is . . .

(& why can we not
stop just there
at

is

that *beauty*

is

being *itself*

can we not stop
there

at the being of
beauty

as if
not light
but the word
beauty
was the first
the alpha omega
first & last

beauty in
beauty out

the genesis
of all
that is

is

everything

everything
is

ipso facto
everything
is
beauty

but we did not
stop

we do not
stop

we go on

to)

. . . nothing . . .

(nothing, nothing

no thing

first & last

that

is)

. . . but the beginning . . .

(in the beginning
the void)

. . . of terror, . . .

(first & last
an eternity of *being*

the keys lost
the knife in the belly
the slow rolling waves
the leviathan
the demons

the ice
breaking
beneath your feet
a bare corner
rocking
a dead
fish
on a carpet
in a tenement
the long loneliness
of madness in a small
room in a city full of lovers
or how you bear your children
turn & turn in the light of your love
imagining only how they can never know
the depth of love until the moment of their deepest pain

yes, yes, say nothing but yes to the angels
someone once said Henry Miller
said yes to everything
that the only thing
not to do was to
say no to the
angels)

. . . that we are still able to bear, . . .

(we bear them
because we

are still

caught in the eternal

beauty

being what we bear)

. . . & we revere . . .

(to respect
to be wary

to be in awe
to look again
to fear the truth of)

. . . it . . .

(das id
the thing
itself
it
self
the it self
of being
beautiful

beautiful:
full of goodness

what is the logic
of any *thing*

Feynman Richard
says infinity
is meaningless

meaning
derives
from
breaking
the whole)

. . . so, because it . . .

(so

because

it

beauty is

it

because

it

is)

. . . calmly disdains to destroy us. . .

(as if creation
alpha & omega
could destroy

what is the logic
of
e (re)ver (e)y(e) thing

as if beauty would offer itself to death
knowing nothing of what the flower knows)

. . . every angel is terror."

(say yes
even as you refuse
the turning of the cry)

[as if the wine resents the grape] *f*

It is your gift to poems that you get out of the way
(all your fears & doubts do not belong to the world
that seeks its way out into the light through you
&, yes, it does, but filtered through a different lens)
just write & the fullness of time will judge
the worth independent of your fears
poems are a gift given through us
like children like laughter
like breath for trees
breathing in images
feelings thoughts & sounds
breathing out poems
is the breath yours? in or out?
is the sky the stars the seas
dreams & landscapes
play before our eyes
& we say: see? look!
here it is:
a kitten in a seashell
a scorpion in lace
these things just turn
& what is the meaning of an image
as grotesque as exquisite as any other
sitting nobly as mesmerizing as a queen
as if you would hide a stranger
found naked at your door
with a face like an angel
no one has ever seen before

[more advice to a poet: just write] *f*

Places where the quiet goes
      where the paint thins
to glass

old gray rocks
not somber
settled

absorbed in its place

amenable to thinness
to tenuous vines
growing brown to green

a sigh in a season

later a constellation
of delicate blooms

or a water that rises from the skin
on warm days then retreats

slowly back to a dream
of a great flat water

she smoothes the curtains
tracing the seam with
her satisfied fingers

this light never intrusive

leans first into the garden
then if she is not ready to turn
it wanders to the courtyard steps

but it never touches
the hallways always
stays behind the windows

an amber curtain of preservation
the world wrapped discreet

in secret places where we dare go
when once the fever of Pandora
strips us of everything

save the need for touch

[the dream of thin connection] *f*

As if to fall
into an identity
were to have blood rush to my face
a name a wanting a cloud like breathing
the birds in a morning green
wet

she stands inside a pool
her hands like wings
where god
sleeps

carry me

as if a dancer
were all the world
released

[identity] *f*

Somewhere
somewhere there is
somewhere there is an emptiness
an emptiness that waits just for you
like a vase for a flower
& it has always been
& it has always
been empty
for you—
you

& when you fill it
it can never
be filled
again

it was an emptiness made only
for you & when you
leave—

when you leave—it will be
an emptiness
again

& forever
& no heaven
can know what
that emptiness knew

when you
left us & we wept—

how we wept for you

wept against this, our long—
our long & starless
emptiness

[& there are emptinesses even tears cannot fill] *f*

So how goes it, you of
the beautiful soul

here i am as if bathed
in river water of
some dream of
imagined
clouds

thinned in honey

meadows
slow soft
eternal

he dreams in irish
(gaelic, aye)
languages
studied
years
ago

(in these towers
made of liquid light)

imperfectly the syntax integrated
(how the watches never catch
even in these prickly
labyrinths)

yet here we speak in silence &
they understand in eyes
like windows, in these
gestures marked
so keenly, so
deeply, so

dreams of bruising tenderness
of turning to eidolons old as memory
how they (these figures played timelessly)
face me quizzically, seeing me suddenly in a different light
& i shifting to see myself as they see me: who came as a child now his hands so

(who was i all those years
who am i become in
the world so wide)

coming to a gentle
consciousness
an awareness
of a place
where
it all
just

amazes

& the beauty astounds
& all the desire folds like a wing for the night

[a letter to some imagined self] *f*

Sweet leaping
the fall
into
who
you will
—become
falling into you

[she remembered an island] *f*

The birds puff in the bare branches
the meager winter berries tremble in the wind
today she brings a blackberry bush
next year or maybe the year after
there will be berries in the fall
& when i gather berries
i will think of small
birds warming
in the quince
or far off
this woman
saying this is it
the road begins here
& there will be sorrow
& in the morning
a joy unlike
any other
she has
ever
been

[berries] *f*

Sometimes
she pretended
to be blind
& in that
alone
she
exceeded
the beauty
of holy saints

or when the old women laughed
she would laugh loudest
& the children of god
would remember
how much Eve
knew of
sorrow

or an island
in a stranger's dream
where the blue of the ocean
is so pure & the waves so very still
that the light becomes a song
& in that moment she is
emptied of regret

or when the boy
saw a bird
on a lake
& she
was
happy

or how
time
floods us
with ghosts
like clouds
suddenly alive
& we remember

how some corner
of a room
became
everything
we ever
thought of
as beautiful
even as it dissolved
like cloudless tears
like a whisper
in the ear
of she
who will
comfort
us all

[what she wanted in clouds] *f*

Reach for anything
not already yours
& why did you

but the flame
the rose

it will not be

how if she surfaces
so very deep

or a red red heat
busted clouds
in the rain
like paper
flowers

what turns always
to ice

her voice like cold daylight
& what touches here
the glass cold
the window
a rose she
suffers

yes & no

remember the wounds
falling crying
clouds of
loss

where the ghosts like sullen brides
the beaches a thousand shells
suffering suffering

who catches the scent

[end here] *f*

He had a bicycle basket full of telephones
black plastic circuits ringing ringing
& he picked them up one by one
& yelled no! no! but they just
kept ringing ringing ring
ing because each ring was a
moment calling the next & the next
& what he did not know was that the voice
on the other end was his voice waiting for him
to make the connection between his life & every thing

[ten lines ringing] *f*

I break

who walks away
who sees me in shadow

the wind—handled leaves wanting to thin

a slip a curtain a cutting of the air

who stands behind the veil
who watches as i peer into this face

who taps on the mirror

that is not me
that cannot be what they see

whose eyes so solemn
whose voice like
a river dying

a tender facade
i am more real in dreams
the child telling me where the mountains
rise in the valley so lost or the silver bartender
with the wooden beard laughing as i pour champagne in the sea
how even a tornado balanced in the palm of my hand
on the wasted industrial landscape of never
knows me better than any human
i have ever held—more even
than the fellow who
calls himself by
my name

[living in the valley] *f*

Listening to the wood thrush
the crisp dry grass
sunlight hiding
in the bough

below the ground
worms like rivers
cut the perpetual
night like pianos
like moonlight
like whales

the waters still in love
with falling

(remember this water
when the sun
roared new)

like a lion of all
that wants burning

[wants burning summer] *f*

Append a name

    —Huxley, Po, Rossetti, Baraka, Kidd—

  a god

    —Hermes, Vishnu, Inanna, Corn Maiden, Death—

    a city

      —Vienna, Xiamen, Perth, Red Deer, Tiruchchirappalli—

        a river

          —Missouri, Congo, Brahmaputra, Elbe, Styx—

a man
on a bed
with a pen hesitates
while a ghost settles into his nerves—

a flesh it knew as the name of a mountain—

or a rain speaking to a bridge on a quiet night—

we hear ourselves called, even as the waters erase the heat of our arriving—

nameless & amazed

[nameless] *f*

I don't look like me i don't sound like me
what you see & what you hear is not me
christ, what i see & hear is not me
who speaks when i open my mouth
who walks in front of the mirror when i do
who writes these words takes this name
i am a thinner man & taller but not so tall
as that man nor as short & when i smile

i have a deeper mouth, a deeper glimmer
i look more amused & my ache is more plain
my longing & shame more visible
how i reach & reach & my failure crushes me

i am a boyish thing behind a screen of gold
some other thing than these fleshy shapes
except my hands, these are my hands
i look just like my turning hands

let me trace along your jaw with my hand
close your eyes my lips at your right ear
breathing softly lips just slightly parted
that is as close as i am to being seen

closer when you smile so faintly
imagining a hand like the breast of a dove
pressed to your cheek as your neck slowly bends—
the scent of oranges heavy in your hair

white sand blue pearl sky
the stars spiraling

i'll be right here
a hand falling
gently away

empty—

having
seen

[having been seen] *f*

f

About the Author

Ric Williams was born in Arkansas in 1952. He began acting and writing early and has been interested in the slippery nature of consciousness ever since. He received his master's degree in mythology and depth psychology from Pacifica Graduate Institute in 1998. Ric has edited the Litera listings of *The Austin Chronicle* since 1988. He wrote the "Poet's Beat" column (interviews with local poets) for *The Austin Light* from 1987-1991. He edited for Ed Buffalo's poetry anthologies *Aileron* and *Vowel Movement* in the late 80's and early 90's and was the associate editor from 1997-1999 for *Alchemy on Sunday*, the literary journal of Pacifica Graduate Institute. He has written and/or edited for the *Austin Chronicle*, *Man! Magazine*, and the *Salt Journal*. He is currently a senior editor for *Creative Pulse Magazine*. His interview with Larry McMurtry is included in *Conversations with Texas Writers*, published in March 2005 by UT Press. This is the first solo collection of his poems. He lives in Austin, Texas, with his artist wife Christy Kale and their daughters Kady and Ramona. "I don't know" is often the wisest thing he has ever said. Yet, he believes the universe is, ultimately, a comedy and wants you to know that, despite any thing you may have heard to the contrary, "You matter. You will always matter." You may contact Ric at thesecretbookofgod@yahoo.com.

Acknowledgments

The author thanks his daughters Kady & Ramona, his niece April Sullivan, his mother Gloria, readers Craig Sullender, Evie Worsham, Kristi Sprinkle, and Judith Pittman. Special thanks to Stephanie Pope for her brilliant editorial suggestions; her always insightful analysis helped shape this book. He also thanks Deltina Hay for her faith; Rod Amis for his indefatigable character; and his wife Christy for this wondrous journey she has so joyfully shared with him; she is still his spring. Vaya con dios.